The

Antidote

Ms. Snakecharma

ISBN: 978-1-7348157-2-6

DEDICATION

This book is dedicated to Hassan Malik. It takes dedication and discipline to be able to succeed in life. The day I dedicated my life to God was the day I started to receive favor. The more I dedicated my life to kingdom principles the more peace and stability I found. I would not have been able to fulfill my dream of becoming a writer without God by my side. I'm thankful for my mother for giving me back to God as a child. From time to time I strayed away but the love from above never changed. Put God first and watch God work.

ACKNOWLEDGMENTS

I want to acknowledge my mother Sugar, as she is affectionately called, for being one of my greatest supporters. If it wasn't for my mother, I would have never known the love that God has for me. I also want to acknowledge my God mother, Suzie Q, for teaching me how to grind early. She taught me so much about these snakes! I also want to acknowledge my sister Nicky and my brothers Boo and Ree. Each of you, and your families, gave me the fuel I needed over the years to keep pushing. Thank you for loving me through it all. I would also like to recognize my partner Mike for inspiring me to be great! You and my amazing son, Malik, are two of my greatest blessings! And finally, the snakes because none of this would have been possible without you!

CONTENTS

CONTENTS

CHAPTER 1

DEFINITION

Charmers are never to be mistaken for snakes. Many believe that you must become what you seek to understand. I agree to a certain extent. I recommend that if you do that, you obtain the knowledge and utilize it to control how you respond to individuals and situations. Prevention is key. If you can identify a snake, or detect a situation that involves snake behavior beforehand, you will be able to finesse what is being presented to work for your benefit. Anyone has the potential to become someone they never intended on becoming. When I realized how powerful self-control was, that's when I became a snake charmer.

Snake charming is the skill to hypnotize a snake by playing an instrument called a pungi. It is a dangerous form of entertainment that was practiced in Ancient Egypt, Southeast Asia, the Middle East and South Africa. Snakes can sense sound, but they lack the outer ear that allows them to hear music. When a snake is being charmed, they follow the pungi that the "snake charmer" holds with his or her hands. The snake considers the person and pungi a threat and responds to it as if it were a predator. Charmers were thought to be magicians and healers. In some religions snakes are believed to be sacred, and believers have them surrounding their gods for protection.

I myself don't believe snakes are sacred. I believe they are cursed. God created all creatures, therefore, I don't hate them. My belief towards snakes were influenced from the bible. In the book of Genesis chapter 3 starting at verse 14, God cursed the snakes. In Psalms chapter 58 verses 3 through 5, wicked people were compared to snakes.

This is how I feel about the entertainment business, too, by the way. My pungi is my mic-and my energy- well, that is hypnotic. Every time I touch a microphone I serve as a potential threat to those who create diversions to distract the sheep. The snakes I encountered throughout my grind don't listen to the music- they utilize it to poison their listeners. These stakeholders profit off those that fiend for fame.

Snakes protect those they worship, which are the ones they rely on to feed them. They do this in fear of starving. Never give anyone the power to control how you eat.

You really can't trust anyone till they give you a reason to. Most times, they will give you a reason not to. Forgiveness is powerful. It's a key characteristic to peace and spiritual growth. Forgiveness does not require forgetfulness. It's intended to plant wisdom and provide insight on the perpetrator's mindset. The fact is, people who snake you aren't sorry until they get caught. Each experience should create awareness.

When you can catch a snake before they bite you, that is the gift of discernment. Discernment is the ability to obtain sharp perceptions. Perception is a skill to see, hear, or become aware of something through energy using your gift of discernment. Discernment is a spiritual gift that is given to the children of God. A righteous skill, that when mastered, gives you leverage.

Many don't understand that God is a universal label that is given to a worshipped being. So, when I utilize the word, I identify it with the Creator of all things. It's important to be mindful that there are many gods created, and many consider themselves a god due to the way they envision themselves. God did create us in His image. However, one of the Kingdom Principles is to never put any gods before the

"Most High". We are supposed to honor one another for good works, but we are not supposed to idolize. Imagine you creating something that takes all your glory and/or aligns themselves with your level of power, skill and creativity. The problem with most people is, they are never satisfied.

Once upon a time, there was a woman in a garden; a serpent convinced her to eat from a forbidden tree. While convincing the woman to eat from the forbidden tree, the serpent left out the part about the garden having many trees that she could eat from, freely. The woman was commanded by God not to eat from that specific tree, but she did anyways.

As children of the Most High, we should carry ourselves like so, but don't get carried away. We also should value ourselves in the same fashion. We reserve the right to have whatever we desire on earth as it is in heaven. These blessings are ushered to us through chosen individuals, situations and experiences that God strategically designs to reach us. It's important to treat everyone you encounter in life with an open mind, because you could be entertaining angels unaware. You could miss out on your blessing being judgmental.

The more we please God, the more we are blessed. This goes for the god of the wicked as well, who many refer to as Satan. You can receive worldly favor for pleasing demonic reinforcers. It goes both

4

ways. That's why you must choose up. Many people struggle with this because they aren't content. If you aren't satisfied with little, you will do almost anything for more. Do remember that, little placed in our Creator's hands becomes much. Exercising faith, practicing patience, exhibiting discipline and walking righteous are pleasing to the Master. The heavenly blessings are more rewarding and never require stepping outside of your character to obtain.

We, the humans, want to be independent, but we are dependent of God. This is the realistic behavior of children. We must learn to be thankful for all things and praise God through all situations.

Religion is complicated because it is man made. Anything that is man made has flaws. Relationships offer more understanding and clarity. The connection with God is the most effective approach to living a righteous life. God will order your steps and provide the best direction. As you build with God, you grow stronger mentally, physically and spiritually.

Snakes are often seen in pictures beside idolized figures as a form of protection. Snakecharmas service the Most High in the same fashion.

CHAPTER 2

EXPOSURE

Hey, not everything is meant to be shared. Some of the knowledge you obtain over the course of life is meant for you, and only you. Snakecharming requires you to be able to keep a secret between you and God. God must be able to trust you with the jewels. You must protect your mind and your heart. Your mind is a treasure. When you have a righteous heart, you are a gem. The wicked come to kill, steal and destroy. They will steal the gems and utilize the light in you to destroy you after. Some of the things you witness are meant to provide you with clarity. The worst thing you can do is share God's plan for you with an opposing force. What God has for you is for you, and only you.

God will give you confidants. Confidants are souls you can trust with your thoughts, emotions, opportunities and etc. If you share your business with the wrong individual, you run the risk of having them use it against you. Most times, they will manipulate the situation; including bits of the truth in a mess of lies that they've created. Learn to keep a secret because some information is sacred.

Some information is lethal. Exposing is an unnecessary risk that can most times lead to death. Wicked people do wicked things. Any publicity is considered beneficial. Exposing can be what they need to get noticed. When you can create awareness by saying less, you become a Snakecharma. Snakecharmas don't have to say much. Snakes eventually expose themselves. Most snakes do not see well, therefore, they will miss the visual you painted for others through your creative way of revealing truth.

For example, when slave masters were planning to sell slaves, the men and women would pretend that they didn't love one another in an attempt to avoid being separated. There is also a story of a righteous man named, Abraham, who introduced his wife Sarah as his sister, to save her from getting killed.

If you absolutely feel the need to let a snake know they are a snake, it's best to go directly to them. You don't need an audience. The after effects of their actions will result in anger, reverse psychology, or self-pity. Reverse Psychology is when snakes make it seem like you are over thinking. Most times, they play victim or catch an attitude. You will also notice that when they get caught, the dynamics change, and conviction settles in. They normally feel bad for you, not for what they did. As I mentioned before, if they would have never been caught, they most likely would still be attempting to snake you. Their goal is to make you think you are insecure or have issues with trust.

Anger is a typical response to humiliation. When someone gets caught up in lies or disloyalty, they become upset. It's embarrassing to know that you couldn't keep it real. Keeping it real requires being real. A lot of people feel the need to "snake it to make it". People fake and front. They try to slither their way in and out of situations for their own benefit. Eventually, they will get tangled up in their own lies or confusion. When you call someone out on their snakey ways, they immediately feel threatened because this could potentially ruin their image.

'Poor me' is another act of reverse psychology. Snakes know your heart. A snake will attempt to go around the situation by highlighting traumatic situations they faced in life. This tactic is used to get you to feel sorry for them. Behavior cannot be excused because of pain that was previously endured. However, it can be expected because people who are in pain cause pain.

It's quite interesting how they act after. Snakes forget the process of healing and rebuilding trust. How do people do you dirty and expect you NOT to use the experience you have with their previous behaviors to prevent more damage from being done? I guess this stems from you being on point and them being slippery. Slippery meaning, slipping up. Slipping is the act of leaving room for mistakes because you are all over the place.

Fact is, snakes are cold-blooded. They feed off good people. They don't have eyelids, so they are always looking for a come up, or outside of what God has already blessed them with. They can't see past their own wants or what God provided them with. Most times they want to eat off you, not with you. Some snakes want to eat you! They want to kill off your projects and/or products.

Snakes respond to movement not sound. You attract snakes when you are going places. They will attack your movement. If they can't destroy your movement, they will mimic your ways. They like to camouflage themselves in your life as friends to absorb as much information as they can. Be careful what you share with them because these slime balls come to kill, steal and destroy. This is why it is important for you to know how to identify a snake. Some of us are chosen to do just that.

CHAPTER 3

CHOSEN

A t times you may feel like you are cursed. When you are destined to do great things, you must overcome great pain. People have a bad habit of blaming God for all the bad that happens in life, because the expectation is that God would never allow bad things to happen to good people. This way of thinking separates you from building an effective relationship with God. Sin caused separation; and we all are subject to sin. If we are not perfect, it's foolish to expect to live in a perfect world. It's wrong to assume that because you trust and believe in God, that you will never have to face the wickedness of the world. The closer you are to God, and the greater your calling is, the more you will be attacked. The snakes don't want what they already have.

Therefore, you must put on the full armor of God. As a godly person, you should expect your faith to be challenged. You should also know that the wicked aren't seeking souls that are lost in the world. Their goal is to convert the righteous. When you are chosen, their goal is to prevent you from fulfilling your mission.

Everything that God does is with great purpose. Sometimes things happen to us to humble us and bring us closer to God. People normally look to God when they need help. Trauma draws people closer to God; forcing you to pray. Maybe God is looking for your attention or maybe God is looking for your testimony.

A testimony is something that is worth sharing. God needs people to witness his power. God has a habit of using people that he knows others can relate to. Your story might be the words he needs another to hear. Your experience could possibly prevent a great number of people from making the same mistake, or provide a perspective to someone who is looking for clarification or confirmation that God is able to do all things.

Most people need to be convinced to believe in something outside of what they can see or feel. Many people need to know they aren't alone and that things could have ended up worst or could be worst. God gives his hardest battles to his strongest soldiers. The enemy uses traumatic situations for his benefit as well. When I say the enemy, I speak of the devil and any forces of darkness that come to stir you away from God. Tough times can cause you to lose faith. When you take losses, it makes you want to give up. Disappointment, failure, betrayal and hardships can lead to depression, worry, or fear. All of which are not of God. The more you build with God, the more prepared you will be. It's important to stay solid and remember you are chosen to do great things.

Death is one of the hardest things to except when you don't understand this is not your home. Once you begin to understand your purpose, and what it means to be alive and not among the dead, then you will cry at birth and rejoice when God calls someone you love home.

The armor of God is mandatory. If you wake up every morning and throw it on, you will be ready for war. It's a war outside. Snakecharmas are warriors!

First you need the helmet of salvation. The "Helmet of Salvation" serves as a protection for your head. An attack to your head could cause you to die instantly. Many people suffer from mental illnesses and don't even know it. If you are going to hold on to thoughts, they should positive. What you think, you become. You must protect your thoughts. You can't just fill your head up with anything and everything. You must learn how to dissect information. Whenever you are taught something, you should want to learn more about it. You should always filter what you take in and remove what's not useful. Mind control is real. If someone can control your mind, they can control your actions.

Feed your brain leafy greens, like kale and spinach, which are rich in brain nutrients like vitamin K, lutein, folate and beta carotene. Walnuts, which resemble the brain, improve memory. Look how detailed God was when he created the fruits and herbs that were designed to naturally heal us. If medicine was designed to heal us, why must we keep filling prescriptions?

The "Helmet of Salvation" is protective gear to deliver you from harm. It's a must for Godly people. You need to protect your thoughts, and keep a clear mindset absent of confusion and chaos.

Next you will need the "Breastplate of Righteousness". A breastplate is worn over your torso to protect it. Your torso is everything between your neckline and pelvis. Your breastplate protects your powerhouse. Your powerhouse is your heart. Spiritual host of wickedness want your heart and soul. Your heart is considered the inner part of the mind; the inner being of a man. What is in our heart determines what we are. Above all things, we are supposed to guard our hearts for out of it flow the issues of life.

Living righteous is practicing good, being noble, conscientious and practicing upright thinking. What you give out you get back. If you walk in righteousness that pleases God and you are rewarded according to your good works.

Your heart is one of the most important organs in your body. Garlic is a miraculous herb that has tons of medicinal properties. Garlic raises good HDL Cholesterol and helps maintain a healthy blood pressure. Cayenne Pepper is also great for your heart. Cayenne contains capsaicin which improves the elasticity of the blood vessels. This spice improves the functioning of the cardiovascular system. Ginger prevents formation of blood clots and Green Tea prevents the risk of Heart Disease.

On your feet you need to be fitted with the "Gospel of Peace". Peace is the absence of destruction. Every day you step out into the world you should be walking in peace, maintaining your peace, keeping your peace, keeping the peace, exhibiting peace and taking peaceful alternatives. Peace is a spiritual reward you receive when you give your life to God. Sharing the gospel is a key component to obtaining peace and you must have it to walk in it. I obtained peace, when I gave my life fully over to Christ and decided to utilize the outline, he provided for man to follow.

Many people don't believe in becoming saved due to the way Christianity has formulated. Historically, we know that the gospel, like many other things, was whitewashed. Man has been known to whitewash meaning to cover up history. The bible has many versions, but like any story being told, the truth is within. Seek and you shall find. When you want to know the facts, you search for them, and I believe that is exactly what God wants us to do. Jesus Christ is referred to by many names. You must get to know him for yourself, and build your own relationship with God, so that you may get the wisdom and understanding. Ceasare Borgia is the man you see in most of the pictures of Yeshua. Educate yourself on the gospel.

Your feet help you maintain balance. When your feet are planted in the truth your chances of being mislead are slim to none. As a Snakecharma, you must learn to stand up for what you believe in and what is right. You can't let anything, or anyone, move you. You must stay solid and be secure in every situation. Don't sell yourself short or compromise your integrity to move forward. You are a leader, not a follower.

Take care of your feet. A great treatment to take care of your feet is to fill a bowl of warm water and add some cinnamon, cayenne and ginger. Let them soak until they are softened. Once your feet are softened use a pumice stone to lightly scrub and remove the dead skin. You can pour baking soda in your sneakers and leave them overnight to remove odors.

The fourth piece of the armor is the "Shield of Faith". The shield of faith protects you from all the fiery darts of the snakes. The shield also covers our heart and body. The shield of faith enforces our trust in God and helps form a stronger protection against these snakes. Faith is having complete trust in God. Faith is the substance of things hoped for and the evidence of things we cannot see. Faith is powerful, it connects us to the spiritual realm which links us to God. If you trust in God, you shouldn't worry or lean on your own understanding of matters. You must let God be God. When you cast your fears and worries on the Lord, he will help you fight your battles. Sometimes victory is won on his time, not ours.

When you are required to exercise your faith, realistically, it may be stressful. You might lose sleep. You may find yourself worrying despite your faith in God. Magnesium is a natural remedy for anxiety. Coconut water, cashews and pumpkin seeds are rich in magnesium. Peppermint is amazing for headaches. Lavender helps calm and soothe your mind. Chamomile Tea also helps calm your nerves. Plenty of rest is essential.

The "Belt of Truth" is another piece of protective gear. The belt also known as the *cingulum* or *balteus* is a very important piece of the armor because it is the belt that holds the scabbard, which is the place that holds the sword. A belt encompasses the waist, conviction to the truth encompasses us. You need a solid belt to keep things in place. Which leads me to the last piece of armor, the "Sword of the Spirit" which is the word of God. In the beginning was the word, the word was with God, and the word was God. The manifestation of the will of God is the word.

Each of us has an important role in the master plan. Once you identify your position you need to be prepared for these snakes to attack. Put on the full armor of God so that you may be able to withstand.

Your body is a temple, which is the dwelling place of God, The God in you is your strength. If we know that cleanliness is next to godliness, then we should know that the cleaner your insides are the more welcoming you are for the Spirit of the Lord. Some of the food we eat is filthy. God created clean food that is good for us. Your kitchen cabinet should be your medicine cabinet.

Rid your body of toxins; synthetic chemicals, processed foods and heavy metals. Genetically modified foods and foods with additives have toxins. Drinking water helps your kidneys remove these toxins. Resting your organs through fasting helps. When fasting, you want to rid your body of alcohol, refined sugar and saturated fats. Also go natural. Minimize the use of chemical based products in your household.

You can detox your body with a smoothie cleanse or a juice cleanse. Cucumber water is great for detoxing. Take plenty Vitamin C because it helps your liver drive out toxins. Herbs that cleanse the liver are dandelion root, burdock and milk thistle. Eat plenty of fresh fruits and vegetables. Eliminate waste through perspiration. You can remove toxins through saunas and foot spas.

God created fruits, vegetables and herbs to keep us healthy! If you eat better, you feel better. Some "Super Foods" are avocados, beans, berries, broccoli, celery, kale and spinach. If you want to eat meat, eat fish. I would recommend salmon. An alkaline diet is extremely healthy.

The measurement of acidity and alkalinity is important when trying to maintain a healthy diet. Alkaline food is healthier than acidic food. The more acid you have in your body, the more prone you are to diseases and sickness. Diseases feed off sugar. Be aware of the PH Levels of the food you're eating. The pH Level's range goes from 0-14 with 7 being neutral. pH Levels less than 7 indicate acidity. Try to drink water with high pH Levels to alkalinize your body as well.

Fasting is refraining from eating at your own will. Fasting has been known to help improve your blood sugar and heart health. When you go without toxic food for about 12 hours, you remove waste from your body. Fasting should be a regular practice, and between you and God. Biblical fasting is a way of humbling yourself before God. The Holy Spirit deals with your spiritual condition. A fast helps you move your focus from your body and toward your relationship with God. When fasting, I recommend you keep it between you and God. When you can maintain your fast in secrecy between you and God, you are rewarded. Fasting leaves you more time for prayer. Prayer is your one on one time with God.

CHAPTER 4

IDENTIFICATION

Recognizing who you are and the potential you have to become is where the transition takes place. We all have the potential to become a snake under the right circumstances or emotions. When you are humble, and understand you can get weak, or make a wrong decision this is when you start to master the art of snakecharming. We all fall short of perfection. Do away with judging others so that you are able to tangle with the snakes and run with the wolves without feeling intimidated or shook. You must be able to walk with all forms of life.

You don't have to snake someone to understand them. You can simply observe their behaviors and take mental notes. The best education is experience. What you take from your experiences helps you to stay on point. If you learn how to identify certain behaviors, you catch a snake before they bite you. You can set traps in advance and have them dancing to your tune. Learn what triggers them, what excites them and what their motives are.

Some of the characteristics of a snake are revenge, hatred, selfishness, pride, narcissism, greed, lust, jealousy and many other toxic poisonous behavior. For example, thieves and liars. If God wanted you to have it, you would have it. People who exhibit these attributes have the potential to snake you. If you want to catch a snake, you simply force their character to receive confirmation. If you want to know if you can trust someone, tell them something you don't mind getting out, and wait to see if they share it. If you want to know if people are genuine, don't let them know what you can do for them in advance.

If you want to find out if they are someone you could count on to have your back, pretend that you are broke. The ultimate test is to say "NO". Some people get use to you saying, "Yes", all the time and once they get a "No", they reveal their true character. The smallest misunderstandings will always show you someone's true face.

Snake bait is using what they lust over to catch them in the act of snaking. Snakes normally have an issue with lusting over things or people. If you give them what they lust over, you can get them to cooperate. For example, many of them can be bought. You can easily get a snake to trade or turn on someone by offering them money.

People who aren't use to having money act the worst over it, but will do the most for it. It's a little more challenging to use money to your advantage for someone who is already familiar with it. You may have to provide an opportunity. People who love and are addicted to money are easily railed in by opportunities. These are your opportunist.

Opportunist disregard principles. They are always looking for an opportunity to advance themselves. This is typical snake behavior. A snake is always trying to get off the ground. Snakes move by pushing off other objects. Always remember that snakes are very selfish, self-centered individuals.

Snakes have a split in their tongues because they tell lies. They can't keep a story straight. They use their tongue to get their prey. They will often use what you say to them and twist it up to destroy you. They love to gossip, to spread rumors, and intake information to create diversions. Their conversations are negative and aren't beneficial.

Snakes leave tracks of where they have been. Their snake behavior is consistent and can be tracked prior to your encounter. They will try to bring others down to bring themselves up. They don't like to be exposed, so they avoid open areas or discussion with people who may know their history. They will come to you talking about someone who isn't even thinking about them to cause friction before you get to know them. Always get to know people for yourself. Your relationship with people should be based on your relationship with people, not a relationship that was established with someone else. You never know the ins and outs of a relationship.

We all tend to make mistakes so even if the information you receive is factual, people do have the ability to change and make self-improvements and better decisions. One of the strongest skills is to love. To show love, to obtain love, to be loved. Love is an action word and is free. Love is about balance, and there are levels and forms to loving. To love your neighbor and exhibit that brotherly love is one of the greatest commandments from the Most High. Snakes love you to death. Once love becomes deadly it turns to hate. Snakes are haters. They love everything about you. They want the love you receive and the love you have for yourself.

Identifying love is vital. Love is patient, kind and doesn't boast. Love does not envy. Love is not proud. Love is not rude, self-seeking, easily angered, and it keeps no record of wrongs.

There are four types of love. The first is "Agape Love" which is unconditional love. This is the highest of all loves. Agape love is a sacrificial, self-less love, like the love God has for us. This type of love could be identified as the love you may have for strangers. It involves taking responsibility for another. The second type of love is "Eros Love". Eros Love is a romantic love. This type of love is an intimate love between two. This type of love is based on physical traits and passion. "Philia Love" is the third type of love, which is between friends, like brotherly love. This is the type of love that builds great friendships. The last is "Storge Love", which is family love. This type of love is the bond between family members; i.e. mother to child.

Snakecharmas have a heart. You must have heart to be on the frontline. You also must have heart to love. "Self-Love" keeps you away from moving like a snake. When you love and appreciate all that you have, and all that God created you to be, you don't feel the need to get jealous or do things to snake the people God has put into your life. Many people who thrive for attention do not love themselves. They look for attention to validate who they are rather than seeking approval through the Creator. If you don't love yourself, you can't love others. If you don't know what love is, you can't love correctly. When you have been disappointed by or deprived of love, you'll have a hard time recognizing or accepting it. In this case you need healing.

Healing comes from God. There is no medication for a broken heart. It takes unconditional love to convince you that love does exist and that you can trust and give your heart to someone or something. Many snakes are broken hearted. They want to cast their pain on others rather than on the Lord. They feel the need to seek revenge and find temporary happiness in seeing others hurt the way they have been hurt.

When you have been hurt you become vulnerable, and snakes' sense that. It's so easy to get bit by a snake when you have a broken heart or spirit. This is when you need God the most. If you don't turn to God for restoration you might turn to the first thing you see to fill that brokenness drugs or even the wrong person. Remember protecting your heart is one of the first lessons to learn.

Another way to identify a snake is when you are at your lowest and highest points in life. If you don't see the same person congratulating you that was there when you were at rock bottom, there is a strong possibility that they are not for you. Snakes love to see you down. They love to pretend like they have your back. Another move they make is to put you in a position where you rely on them, and then once they know you are, they turn around and make themselves unavailable. They want to see you stuck, and they find pleasure in knowing that you needed them.

If you take something from a snake, make sure you are prepared to have them share what they have done for you. People who feel the need to tell people of the good works they do, aren't doing it from the heart.

Make sure you aren't one of them, or are in danger of becoming one of them. Remember what it means to love. When you feel yourself stepping outside of those attributes, you are becoming one of them.

We all can do so under the right circumstances.

When you give, make sure you are not giving for recognition. Refrain form bragging about what you do, unless you are using it to encourage others to do so or setting an example on how it should be done.

When someone trust you with information, honor your word and keep that information to yourself. You should be able to keep a secret even if you fall out with the person you share the secret with. Your loyalty should not be based on your current situation.

When someone loans you something, make sure you return the favor with the same energy you carried when you needed a hand. Snakes often create conflict when they can't repay you or don't want to. Pay your debts. And if someone owes you, don't go hounding them down. If they owe you, you will never go broke. If you don't have it to give, don't give it, because you won't know when you will get it back, or if you might get it back. If you are helping someone understand that it takes time to get back on your feet so it may take time for them to give you back or get you back.

Lastly, don't take advantage of anyone helping you. That is snake behavior. If someone attempts to use you, or happens to use you, don't seek revenge. You will be rewarded by God for your good works. Don't do things expecting a reward but you can expect a reward when you don't seek revenge.

CHAPTER 5

CONTROL

Maintain control. If you can learn to control your emotions, you will learn to control situations. For every action there is a reaction. Every situation doesn't require your attention or reaction. If you act like a clown you become part of the circus. Some situations are simply beneath you. Remember you are royal and must think like so. The best form of revenge comes from God, and when people persecute you or harm you, God takes offense to this. The worst thing a snake can do is to do harm to God's children.

When you catch a snake, you don't always need to let them know. For example, if you feel like your spouse is cheating, and find out they are, you can gather more information by not responding right away. Snakes will deny everything and try to lie their way out of trouble. You can't rely on the person that they are cheating with to be honest, either. They will either lie for your spouse in an effort to convince them of their loyalty or they will make up more lies mad at the fact that they may be getting kicked to the curb.

What you seek you will find. If you aren't ready for the pain that comes with finding out someone you love isn't loyal, then don't look for anything. Most likely, if you feel it, then it's real. Pray about it and God will put things into perspective more clearly. Being cheated on is painful, and it can cause you to act out of character. But remember, that shows a lot about the other person's character, not yours. Not everyone is loyal or is trustworthy.

Discipline is maintaining your cool in difficult situations. A difficult situation could be when you're being provoked. On the flip side, you could be in a relationship and be tempted by the opposite sex. You most likely won't be able to maintain self-control if your mind isn't right. If you are constantly engaging with the opposite sex, entertained my sexual content, or looking outside of your relationship at explicit content, you are filling your brain with lust. You are feeding the demon. What you think, you become, and what's on your mind and in your thoughts, you want or yearn for.

If you are single, you should have a set of expectations for anyone

31

who you allow in your temple. When you truly love yourself, you will not want to share yourself with anyone because you value and know your worth. Your body isn't for everyone, and when you respect it, you won't share it with everyone. You should not be accessible to everyone. Some people just have no self-control. They are loose and all over the place. People who are all over the place are a mess. No matter how they polish up outside, their inside is tarnished.

Loyalty and trust go hand and hand. A part of being real is walking in truth. Winners don't have to cheat. They can be trusted to end up on top regardless of what comes against them.

Defend yourself by any means necessary. Many people think because you have a good heart that you are soft. You are "Saved" by God's grace, but you can't be running around here soft. God didn't give us the spirit of fear. He gave us the spirit of a sound mind. To have a sound mind means you can seek God, filter the thoughts in your head, adjust your emotions and make decisions that are based off your mind not the matter. It's mind over matter. "Mind Over Matter" reminds you to use your head and to control the events that might transpire. Don't let anyone physically harm you, always defend yourself. Use your knowledge to "Know the ledge". Know the ledge so you don't fall off track into the pits of ignorance. Wisdom is broken down into two words "Wise and Dome"; wise your dome. A wise person can control all that comes in his/her circumference.

Mind control is important for you to maintain, and is a goal for almost every snake. Mind control is psychological influence. However, mind control can be used for good or for bad. In business, mind control is a marketing tool. You will have more success by thinking for them. When you set things up for clients and make things easier, you will get the buy in and results you want. Most humans are lazy and love when you do things for them. If you set it up, you are in control. Ask for the inch before you ask them to take the mile. You want to inch your way into someone's favor. You want to spoon feed them. You want people to be able to digest what you are offering. When you believe in what you are trying to sell, you don't beg, you simply demand. Don't make it about the money, because this convinces others that it's crucial. When you are attempting to control someone's mind you never ask them to think it over.

The world has developed technology that is designed to read your mind to advertise products and services that they think you may need or want. A lot of the applications we install on to our devices require permission to our data base which includes our contacts, files, emails, message, pictures and etc. We also accept cookies, which is data sent to you from a website to be stored on your computer. Cookies are designed to remember stateful information and record your browsing history. Whenever you search for something that information is recorded. This information helps filter the ads you receive. This is a form of mind control. It's important to erase the cookies and uninstall applications from your phone, daily, to avoid your personal information being stored and used against you.

When people have control of how you eat, where you sleep, and how you get back and forth, you give them power to control your next move. Assistance is great, but when you rely on a system, person, place or thing you become dependent on them. You won't be able to survive if they no longer decide to support you. Some help enables us from reaching our potential. You should never get comfortable with any form of assistance.

Another form of control is when you do something in secrecy with a snake. Examples of this are when you step outside of your character for a reward, when you do things that could potentially destroy your character, or compromise your freedom. When a snake wants you to cooperate, or gets upset with you, they will hold this over your head. Snakes will have you do something awful to obtain leverage.

Controllers love to get into your head to create fear and worry. Guard your mind, your life flows from it. Make sure to meditate on proverbs so they are stuck in your head. Monitor your thoughts, and when your mind drifts off, regain your focus by speaking truth against error. Write things down, recite them so you can abstain from the things polluted by idols. Maintaining self-control requires a clear, sober mind.

CHAPTER 6

CHARM

A charm defined is power. There are many types of charms and many people think of it as a form of attraction or good luck. Psychologist, Dr. Iris Pachler, describes a charming person as someone who can be okay even when external factors, such as the surroundings and environment. Someone with charm is able to find peace and strength from within with the ability to be flexible and accepting no matter the situation.

Charm is a form of manipulation. The act of manipulating a snake in a skillful manner is the gift of a Snakecharma. Manipulation can be used in a bad way, but Snakecharmas use it to maintain control in snakey situations. Snakecharming doesn't require magic, nor is about luck. Snakecharming relies on discernment and its use to maintain the upper hand in this snakey world. Snakecharmas are admirable, attractive, unique, peaceful, impressive, expressive, actual, majestic, persuasive, peculiar, mysterious, compassionate, strong, bright, natural, sensual, graceful, dreamy, undeniable, extraordinary, powerful God fearing and pleasing people.

CHAPTER 7

SNAKES

Snakes are also called serpents. Snakes are part of the legless species of reptiles. They lack external limbs, movable eyelids and external ear openings. All snakes are predators. Snakes are coated with and identified by their colorful patterns. Snakes shed their skin as they begin to grow. This process is called molting. Snakes are cold blooded creatures. They need light to raise their body temperature. They need warmth to grow. Their body adapts to the temperature around them. Snakes spend the most of their life resting and finding food. Snakes are classified as harmless while others are considered dangerous.

The dangerous snakes are known as Venomous Snakes. Venomous Snakes inject toxin into their victims when they bite them. The poison is released through their fangs. The **Black Mamba**, **King Cobra** and the **Rattle Snake** are popular Venomous Snakes. Venomous Snakes are often referred to as "Poisonous Snakes". A **Garter Snake** often referred to as Garden Snake is a Poisonous Snake because some species possess a mild neurotoxic venom. Garter Snakes can absorb the toxins of other poisonous creatures. Unlike other Venomous Snakes the Garter Snake is considered harmless.

The **King Cobra** is the longest venomous snake in the world. This is the snake that is captured and used by Snake Charmers. The word "cobra" means hooded. Some cobras have spots on the back of their neck to resemble eyes to make themselves look more intimating from behind. King Cobra's spread their hoods and growl when they feel threatened. Another interesting facts about King Cobras is they eat other snakes. In addition to that they are the only species of snake that build their own nest and unlike most snakes King Cobras will defend their eggs. However, they take off on their babies once they are born.

Some snakes are sold in snake trades. **Pythons**, being one of the largest, non-venomous snakes are the most popular snakes to be sold and traded. Their unique pattern on their scales is often used by designers for purses, belts and other accessories. The **Boa Constrictor** is another non-venomous snake that is sold and traded. Boa Constrictors unlike most snakes give birth to live babies. Their eggs are carried inside of the mother until they are ready to hatch. Boa Constrictors are named after the process they use to kill their prey which is by squeezing them to death. The **Anaconda** is also a member of the Boa Family and one of the largest snakes in the world. All these snakes are categorized with the group of deadliest snakes in the world.

The **Viper** is another dangerous snake distinguished by its fangs. A

Viper can open its mouth up to 180 degrees to bite its prey. The Vipers long fangs allow it to decide on how much venom it wants to inject in its prey. Vipers are found all over the world and can look very different.

The **Rat Snake** is a unique snake. They Rat Snake releases a smelly odor when feeling threatened. These snakes are known to slither away when they sense danger. When they are approached by another snake, they rattle the end of their tail to fool other snakes into believing they are venomous.

Another interesting snake is the **Water Moccasin** also known as the "Cotton Mouth" Snake because of the white color inside of the snake's mouth. Water Moccasins are venomous snakes with a dangerous bite that love the water. These snakes are often mistaken for the **Water Snake**. The Water Snake is harmless. The end of the tail of a Water Moccasin is black and that is how you distinguish the two.

There are over 3000 different species of snake in the world. I highlighted some of the most popular to familiarize you with some basic information. Outside of the information I provided you should know these interesting facts.

Snakes are carnivores which are meat eaters. They can't chew their food therefore; they swallow their food whole. Their jaws can expand larger than their head allowing them to eat larger prey. There are approximately 750 Venomous Snakes and out of those 750 snakes 250 can kill a human with one bite. Snakes kill over 40,000 people a year.

The warmer the body of a snake is the faster it can digest its prey. It normally takes 3 to 5 days for a snake to digest food, but an Anaconda which can devour a jaguar could last up to weeks. Most snakes kill their prey by constriction, but the remainder utilize their fangs. When snakes' fangs wear out new ones grow into place.

Snakes have very poor eyesight, they respond to movement, which often startles them. Snakes cannot cry, and they can only see shape but not detail. Snakes rely on their sense of smell to identify prey. The Snakes forked tongue allows them to pick up scents.

Venom is toxic. Venom destroys and/or disrupts your nervous system. There are four types of venom; proteolytic, hemotoxic, neurotoxic and cytotoxic. The only way to treat a snake bite is with an antidote. An antidote is a remedy to counteract the effects of a poison.

I intentionally shared some details on the species of the snake and the anatomy in effort to broaden your perspective on the human snakes in society. There are many types of toxic people that we encounter in life. Many of which possess the same characteristics of the snakes I mentioned.

The Black Mamba

The Black Mamba is the fastest known snake. They also bite their prey numerous times. Unlike most snakes these venomous predators are found in pairs or small groups. I like to compare them to groups of wicked people. A team of snakes! When dealing with these types of snakes you must be prepared to get attacked from numerous angles because they have multiple individuals to attack you. When you are dealing with multiple enemies you are subject to being bitten quicker. A Black Mamba could relate to a group of colleagues or competitors. They all share the same interest which is to attack you. These are the type of people that snake one another one day, but are friends the next. They will work together to defeat you even if they don't get along because they hate you so much.

The Black Mamba's want to know what you do and how you do it. They mimic your style rather than give you credit and admit you inspire them. They will critique what you do but they never provide edible feedback. When they talk about you to others, they only mention your flaws or mistakes. They sneak diss you but come to you in secrecy for assistance. Their overall goal is to distract you from being great. They are the type of people to come up with problems but never have solutions. They love to create drama among you and others. They are incompetent, so they dissect your work in hope to find errors to take the attention off them.

The Black Mamba will give you thanks and recognition when others are not around, but won't when there is an audience because they talk about you to these same individuals. Your real friends and supporters won't have any issues with showing you love in front of others.

The Rattle Snake

The Rattle Snake is a venomous snake that rattles and hisses. Their venom is extremely potent. Their bites leave you bleeding eternally. The Rattle Snakes make a lot of noise, but they aren't about nothing. These individuals like to gossip and spread lies. Rattle Snakes run from person to person carrying information, so be careful what you share with them. Their goal is to shake things up. They normally start the conversation with "did you hear" or "have you heard"? They are like news reporters- they never have the facts straight. These snakes chop and screw up the truth to hold up a conversation. These are the people that ask a million questions.

Never share your secrets with anyone who talks to you about everyone. Anyone who talks to you about everyone else talks to everyone else about you. If they come to you with information that someone else said about you disregard that info because if they were your real friend, they would invite you to the conversation.

These snakes are toxic! Their bites cause internal bleeding. The power of the tongue is lethal and could scar you internally. If you don't want your personal business blasted when they get upset, or shared with opposing forces for their own benefit don't carry long intimate conversations with them.

These crafty story twisters will premeditate on lies. When they know they are beginning to get caught up and tangled up they will plant a person, place or object ahead of time into the picture to make their story seem creditable. They will insert a fact into their tale or mention something that is identifiable to convince others that they are speaking the truth.

When you keep it real you don't need to explain yourself or provide supporting evidence. The truth has a way of revealing itself through the mistakes of a fraud. A fraud will always slip up. Remember you can fake being real, but you can't be real and fake.

The worst enemy that a liar has is someone with a strong memory. Liars can't keep up with their own lies because one lie leads to another.

The Garter "Garden" Snake

The Garden Snake is one of the most common snakes. They are everywhere and come in many colors. The Garden Snakes are not venomous, but they give off a foul smell when threatened. These snakes are found in your backyard. The Garden Snake is the snake that you must make sure you keep your grass cut for. These are the people in your life who you would most likely do the most for. These are the pillow talkers, bed bugs, people who run from house to house with baggage and negative vibes.

These snakes will do anything to get in your circle. They will offer you things they have to make you feel like they care. For example, have you ever had a friend or family member give you something or do something for you, then the minute you stop talking they run around and tell everyone they did this and that for you? These people are secretly jealous of you. They want to feel like they are putting you on. They wait for the moment to put you on blast. They want to feel like they contributed to the love you receive from others and that it wouldn't be possible without them.

These people will intentionally destruct your property or belongings. They will take things with no intention of returning them. They will steal from you, and they'll even have the nerve to come around with what they stole at times. They are so forgetful. They forget they stole from you! They take advantage of you because you let them in your home. Your home meaning your house, your temple (body), your place of comfort. Everyone shouldn't be invited into your home. Not everyone deserves to know where you rest at.

Garden Snakes are the worst because they are everywhere. They always have something to say about the way someone else is living or surviving. Anyone who has time to focus on others is not focused on themselves. We all have areas of our lives we can improve on. Garden Snakes will spend more time on examining others than working on their own imperfections. This is the main reason why they don't really get ahead.

They will paint a beautiful picture to make you believe they are doing well because they need validation from others to feel successful. Remember, the grass isn't always greener on the other side. Sometimes it just appears that way.

Pythons

Pythons can be bought! Pythons are the disloyal snakes. They trade will trade on their own momma. They will sell you out for a bag of designer clothes that don't even fit. Everything they do is to benefit themselves. They are always looking for a come up. Pythons are moved by money.

The worst type of python is one that doesn't have money, so they get around it, or see it, and don't know how to act. They get so excited! When you bring these type of pythons around money, they turn in to experts. They won't shut up. They know everyone and everything. These are the type of people who mention other people's names as a character reference. They will tell all the business, all the plans, and all the ideas just to fit in.

You should never be the smartest person in the room or the person always talking. It's always best to be quiet and learn whose who and the order of operations. Observe and analyze people and environments. Snakecharmas adapt to any situation.

Pythons will sell their soul. This means they will compromise their relationship with others, and more importantly God, for an advancement. They will step out of bounds to score. For example, if they are told they need to bark like a dog on all fours for a promotion, they will. Pythons rock with whoever is winning at the time. They disregard principles, boundaries, respect for themselves, and standards when making decisions.

These serpents ride other people's waves and will sell you up the river to stay afloat. They won't paddle with you in the storm but they will sip lemonade with you in the shade under the sun.

They are also very insecure. The worst thing you can do is share your wealth or spotlight with someone other than them. They will do everything in their power to tarnish your relationship with others because they fear someone interfering with their relationship with you. They are threatened by anyone who they feel could reap the benefits of being attached to you. They will make it seem like everyone you meet is no good for you.

Phytons will act like you belong to them and only them. They aren't in love with you, they are in love with what you can do for them. Anyone who loves you loves to see you get the love you deserve from all faucets of life. They will not try to keep you caged or boxed in. Anyone who is keeping tabs on your movements, watching your pockets and clocking your activities, is overstepping their position in your life.

Phytons are the people you can't say no too. These are the people who get comfortable with you doing everything for them, and then nervous and aggressive when you don't. They are the folks that won't pull out no money in a drive thru but will order everything on the menu at your expense. They are selfish, self-centered and dependent on others.

However, there has been some rare cases of pythons having it all and still exhibiting some of these behaviors. Some pythons have it all and still aren't happy. They want to align themselves with you because you reflect the energy they yearn for. They want to keep up with you to make sure you don't surpass them. Money and possessions come and go! You can't put a price tag on loyalty, peace, love and respect. Materialistic people don't know the value of such things.

Boa Constrictor

The Boa is another trader! The Boa shares many of the same

characteristics of the Python expect the Boa constricts you. These are your friends that hug you and dap you up (be careful who you hug and shake hands with because this is how demons soak up your energy and shift). To best understand a constrictor, you need to understand what it means to constrict. To constrict means to cut off the flow.

Boa's want to cut off your current. They don't necessarily want what you have. The Boa just wants to prevent you from having it. They attempt to get as close as possible to you. Their goal is to learn your weaknesses. Then they use your weakness to suck the life out of you.

They don't work with you, they are working against you. They want to be a part of everything to cause confusion and chaos. They offer their assistance at a time when you need it most only to screw you over. These slimes come to stultify your mission.

The Viper

The Vipers are your most toxic group of people. These are the ones that leave deep scars. Everything they say, do and think is negative. When they bite you, they cut deep and inject emotions like depression, stress, suicide, hopelessness, fear, worry, anxiety, doubt, sadness, discouragement and many others that are deadly if not treated.

The Viper carries a lot of toxins with them and transfers them to others. Many times, they don't know they are toxic because they have yet to identify and admit they are suffering. To truly help a Viper you must start at the root of where their pain stems from. Vipers are not necessarily bad people, they are hurt people who hurt people. These are the people that you pour into, but they never pour back because they are empty. When you are a good person you naturally want to help people. Vipers need fixing that you can't provide. They need internal healing that may have stemmed from a traumatic loss or experience.

Many Vipers suffer from addictions. The disease controls the way they think, their moods, and how they respond to situations. It's important to understand that when dealing with a Viper, you are not dealing with the individual you are dealing with the disease. Vipers often act out of emotions. They have little to no self-control, and they hardly ever take accountability for their actions.

They can't take care of others because they can't take care of themselves. You really can't expect anything from them but disappointment. These are the people you allow to hurt you repeatedly, and give multiple chances to out of love. The best thing you can do for a Viper is to pray with them and for them. You also need to find forgiveness so that you won't develop some vengeful behaviors.

Vipers will leave you weak if you allow them to. You must stay strong and consistent with prayers. Your prayers could be saving them from destruction. The minute you stop praying might be the moment the devil is able to defeat them. Build them up as much as possible. To build is to elevate them mentally by adding a positive spin to their negative. Don't allow the negativity to outweigh the positivity.

The Rat Snake

The Rat Snake is an interesting snake. The Rat is the snitch. The snitch that is down for the cause till they get caught. The one who knows about something and won't mention it until they get disappointed in the individual. The one who wants to expose corruption or criminal activity after the fact.

The best way to avoid them is to keep your business to yourself. Do your dirty work by yourself because you're the only one who could tell on you. Better yet don't do anything that you wouldn't do with others watching. The truth is, the streets have eyes and the walls have ears. There is so much technology out now that is equipped to monitor our lives that it's almost impossible to get away with anything.

Every time you download an APP, or allow your location to be used to complete the installation of the application, you are sharing your personal information, and those who are in your phone. For example, you give them the consent to have access to your pictures, texts, contacts, emails and messages. The best way to secure your information is to uninstall applications after using them. Never save your passwords to sites. Make sure you delete the cookies and caches out your devices, daily. A private life protects your business, family and relationship.

The Rat Snake is not your honest civilian. If someone is violated and is not in the streets, and they tell on something that effects their livelihood, they are not a snitch. Snitching is when you are participating or have participated, cooperated and/or agreed to do something. Then when you get caught up, you tell. You must know the difference before labeling someone a snitch. A snitch is a dangerous name to throw around with out any evidence. Make sure your fact check is accurate and official.

The Rat Snake rattles its tail to portray themselves as something they are not when they feel threatened. Rats aren't built for the mess they get themselves in to. Many people think its okay to hang with a Rat because they weren't the one who wasn't ratted on. Don't slip up and trust one or get mixed up with one because then you become guilty by association.

The Anaconda

The Anaconda is considered a water boa and is one of the heaviest snakes in the world. The Anaconda constricts and drowns its prey in the water. They swallow their meals whole and after they do, you normally won't see them for weeks.

I like to identify the takers as the Anacondas. These are the greedy individuals who eat off you and bounce. The ones that show up to your house without a dish. It's rude to show up empty handed! They just want, want, want. You don't hear from them until they need something, and if you need something, they are no where to be found.

These are the people that you loan something to and must ask for it back. Most times they create an argument or conflict because they don't have it to return. Always return what people loan you with the same energy you had when you asked for it. Never loan out anything you can't afford to lose because there is no telling whether or not you will ever see it again.

Anacondas burn their own bridges before crossing them. They will drown you with their issues to gain your sympathy. They love vulnerable, naïve, reliable people. They aren't here to destroy your reputation or end your career, they just want your hand from time to time, and you better not say no.

The Water Moccasin

Water Moccasins males do a combat dance to decoy females away from males. The males fight over the females and the winner gets to mate with the female moccasin. I like to relate these snakes to anyone who gets vicious over the opposite sex.

Have you ever had someone you trusted sleep with your man or woman? Have you ever dated someone who slept with a friend or family member of yours behind your back? Water Moccasins, the people who will betray you to get wet! If that makes any sense to you. Just extra horny! No self respect or discipline.

First, you should never let another man or woman live in your house with you and your spouse. The opposite sex in your home has the potential to stir up hormones. That walk from the room to the shower in a night gown or them observing you being intimate with your companion could cause their imagination to wander.

Second, you should never brag about what your man or woman does to you sexually. People are naturally curious and if you keep sharing your experience with others, they may want a taste. You shouldn't be talking about your spouse, good or bad, with anyone. Talk to your spouse instead. Let them know how great they made you feel or how much you enjoy the things they do.

Third, never be comfortable with sharing your temple with multiple people. If you decide to be with someone who is in a relationship, it shows a lot about your character. It's like you don't mind being second, or you're not good enough for all. When you don't have no respect for your own body others won't either. Everyone they are intimate with, you are also intimate with. You really must know your worth, and set the tone and boundaries with people, especially someone who you allow inside you or vice versa.

Fourth, fighting is foolish. You can fight for something/someone you love, but you should never have to fight over something/someone you love. Anyone who loves you is not going to allow you to make a fool of yourself or put you in position to fight. Always address your man or woman with a conflict, not the other individual. You can never trust someone who is on the sideline to be honest with you or respect your feelings. Why would you fight someone who may have been getting lied to also? Don't be that man or woman who accepts being second! If we all set standards and refuse to participate and condone cheating, it may not exist.

Lastly, don't entertain the opposite sex when you are in a relationship. People always cheat with the people they say they aren't attracted to. That guy who disrespects females but has money to spoil you. That naked female with fake body parts who shares with the world.

Who you lay down with should be a reflection of your soul. Love is a beautiful thing. Don't get excited off that wet wet.

The King Cobra

The King Cobra is the snake that is typically used in snake charming.

An interesting fact about The Cobra is that it eats other snakes. This is the only snake that can eat other poisonous species. A King Cobra can bite and kill a human in less than an hour. Cobras hiss, spit and growl. Their venom is very dangerous and deadly.

The King Cobras are the people in power. You must know what makes them move, then get them to rock to your rhythm. In business there are really no friends. Most people in business will bite their own partners head off never mind yours.

Be an active listener. Listen to learn. The best form of communication is listening. The more you listen, the more you learn about others and their way of thinking.

Negotiate. Everything is a negotiation. Every conversation you hold is a negotiation. When you talk to someone you are intending to get them to agree with what you say. When you are conducting business always go in with a plan on what you want out of it. Once you establish what you want shoot for more; that way you make sure to get what you wanted.

Entertain is the root word in entertainment. Many of these platforms are looking for individuals to entertain the things that they find humor or excitement in; sex, drugs and violence typically gets more views. The entertainers never make as much money as the people who hire them. Normally, they are instructed on how to perform or execute a task to deliver the entertainment to a controlled audience.

You can't get your emotions wrapped up with these snakes. You must always keep a straight face and move with a strategic plan to accomplish your goal. You must thoroughly think things through. Consider the pros and cons (the good and the bad) in every situation. You may also want to test your processes and projects with a variable (which is something or someone who is liable to change).

Anything that you are passionate about should be taken seriously, and should be utilized to express how you feel not others. There is no amount of money or level of fame that should allow you to change who you are or what you believe in. Anything that God has destined for you will not compromise your soul. Utilize your talents and gifts to uplift others, and you will be lifted by God.

Be patient. The blessings that God has for you verses what the world has to offer requires preparation. God must be able to trust you with certain blessings, because some people, when they get ahead, forget where they came from and they forget their mission. Money isn't the root to all evil, it's the people who do evil to obtain money. A humble, content spirit and mind unlocks bigger blessings.

Don't let people use you for their own entertainment. Instead, learn how to make them move to your beats!

THE ANTIDOTE

Snake bites are dangerous; some are minor, most are lethal and deadly. Prevention is the best defense mechanism. However, if you let your guard down and get bitten, you must know how to treat the wound and ease the pain.

Identification

Identifying what bit you is the first step. You should always learn from your mistakes. Revisit the scenario and find out where you went wrong. Once you find out where you went wrong, find out what you could have done better. Experience is better than education. Don't be so hard on yourself for the mistakes you make in life. Mistakes breed knowledge. Learn to take losses with your head held high. The only time your head should be down is when you are praying to the Most High.

Acceptance

Acceptance is the second step. Accept the fact that you made a mistake and that you are not perfect. Accept change. Change allows a new perspective on things. Change requires risk. Many people are afraid of the unknown. A risk is taking a chance on something without knowing the outcome. Why not take the risk for yourself? Are you not worth it? You may need to change your plans, the people you associate with, the places you go, your environment, the way you eat and drink, and your intake; meaning the food you eat, music you listen to, or what you're watching. Accept responsibility and be accountable for decisions and choices you make. Own up to your mistakes. Accept the things you can't change, the things that won't change and the situations you have no control over.

Accept advice, edible feedback (feedback that is good for your soul), apologies, and the consequences that came with your actions. Accept the time it will take to build yourself back up physically, mentally and spiritually. Accept the resources and people that are dedicated to support you or your situation. God will usher people into your life to help you get through tough times. It's important to be mindful of the people you encounter in life because you could be entertaining angels.

When I accepted Christ (Yeshua) into my life, I found instant peace. All I had to do was open my heart and mind, and I asked God to forgive me. At the time, I had many conflicting thoughts regarding religion, so I begged God to reveal the truth to me. I wanted to learn who Christ was and why his name was so significant. I felt the need to know his real name and origin. I wanted clarification on why there were so many bibles and translations.

How could I trust in what I could not see, touch or feel? How could I just accept what I was told? I humbled myself, got on my knees and asked God questions. This is when I felt the presence of the Lord and things were revealed to me. Things that, if I were to share with others, they would not understand. In addition to this, I accepted Christ as my

Savior. Immediately after accepting him, I felt the Holy Spirit. The Spirit of the Lord provided comfort.

As I began to study the life of Christ, and to study his teachings, the more things begin to change for me. I wanted to prepare a comfortable space for the Spirit of the Lord to reside, so I began cleansing my body. Once the Spirit of the Lord is within you the wickedness begins to flee. I obtained peace, wisdom and clarity. Before becoming a Christian, I was walking in darkness and battling demons, but when I called on the lord, I was saved. If you, too, would like to be saved, I included the sinner's prayer below. Simply, say it with your mouth and believe it by faith with your heart. Do not feel obligated to do so. Whatever path you take to build a relationship with God is respected. I'm just sharing mine.

"Dear Lord Jesus, I know that I am a sinner, and I ask for your forgiveness. I believe you died for my sins and rose from the dead. I turn from my sins and invite you to come into my heart and life. I want to trust and follow you as my Lord and Savior".

Many people base their relationship with God on what they've been taught, or heard, rather than seeking understanding from the source. If you pray to the Most High, I believe you will get what you are seeking for. My life changed drastically when I made that commitment to walk with Christ. Christ outlined what a righteous life consists of.

I took it upon myself to build with other individuals who loved the Lord to learn what they felt pleased God. Only because I wanted to please God more. It seems like the happier God is, the more blessed, safer and secure you become. I learned about the commandments and promises God made. Everything I learned I prayed on, and asked God to show me a sign if it was meant for me, or not. I feel like some things aren't for everybody, and I wanted God to maintain control of what was appropriate for me. It was important for me to build my own relationship with him, and focus on that, rather than the relationship others had with him.

Like many others, I battled controlling my emotions. I held so much in due to embarrassment, pride and hurt. I was getting blessed and doors were opening. The truth is, they were opening for me prior, but before there was always something evil attached to it. The advantages I have now don't require me doing anything out of character. I didn't have to compromise my soul or loyalty to obtain them. The devil rewards you, too! I learned the difference when I cleaned up my mind and body. I could see things for what they were; clearer without the smoke fogs. How did I find peace?...

Forgiveness

Forgiveness is how I obtained peace. Letting go of things, people, places, events, outcomes, bad memories and traumatic experiences brought me peace. If you don't let go you can't move ahead; holding on to things holds you back. Find forgiveness for people, the same forgiveness you will want to receive from others or God for your mistakes. Forgiveness doesn't require you dealing with the individual again. Forgiveness doesn't mean be a fool. Never forget what was done or let your guard down. A snake that strikes once will most likely strike again, and if it slithers and hisses like a snake, it's a snake! A zebra doesn't change its stripes, nor does a leopard change its spots. Call it what it is, forgive and let go.

Living in the past prevents you from having a life in the future. You can't change yesterday. Make the best of every new day and remember tomorrow is not promised.

Forgive yourself for being imperfect. Once you realize you make mistakes you learn to forgive others easily. Ego tripping will have you smiling on the outside and leaking internally.

Self-Care

The next step is self-care and self- awareness. Self-care involves taking care of you and finding out your triggers. A trigger is something that brings you back to the place of your original trauma. Triggers are things that remind you of things you are trying to remove out of your life. Whenever you are trying to stop doing anything whether it is an addiction, habit or emotion you need to know what triggers you. If you know that you love chocolate, you may want to avoid going to the candy section in the store for a while. If smoking is an issue in your life think about the things that make you want to smoke because those are triggers. Avoid hanging around smokers for some time till you can fully rid the urge to smoke. Refrain from going places where they smoke a lot till you are disciplined enough to resist and control your desire to smoke.

To break an old habit or behavior create a new habit in its place. Scientist believe that it takes about 21 days of consistent conscience effort to create a new habit and to break an old habit.

Self-care is taking time for you. Give yourself permission to take a time out from the world. Self-care is a priority. When you prioritize your daily agenda set aside some time for you.

Make sure to get plenty of rest. Even God rested when creating the world. God wants us to rest periodically from our labor. Sleep deprivation will kill you faster than food deprivation. Sleep improves your memory, extends your lifespan, boosts your creativity, sharpens your attention, helps your body naturally heal, and strengthens your immune system. Its recommended that you have a minimum of 6 hours of sleep and a maximum of 8 hours a sleep a day. God also speaks to you through dreams!

Self-care also involves eating right and exercising. God created food to naturally heal our bodies and prevent us from sicknesses and diseases. Your kitchen cabinet should be your medicine cabinet. Consider an alkaline diet. An alkaline diet outlines food that helps you reduce the acid in your body. Acid is harmful. You can change the body's pH levels by eating certain foods. The pH scale measures how acidic or alkaline something is on a scale of 0-14. Something that is alkaline is on the basic end of the scale, or greater than 7. For example cancer cells thrive in acidic environments. Acidic environments have a low pH. Therefore if you eat alkaline foods and limit acidic foods, you can raise the body's pH levels and this will help you prevent getting cancer.

The food we eat has a huge impact on our inside and outside. Periodically remove dairy, sweets and meat out of your meals for a couple days to cleanse your system. If you go without meat make sure you eat energy boosting foods. You need to make sure you are still getting protein and fiber. Salmon is great! Beans, lentil and chick peas are also great choices.

Just like you grease the outside of your body make sure you grease the inside, too! Educate yourself on essential oils, teas and herbs that help cleanse and detox your body. I offer tons of tips on my "Garden of Eden" blog on my website: www.snakecharma.com.

Pamper yourself. Make sure you feel good about you! Take yourself out. Buy yourself things you like. Get your hair and/or nails done. Appreciate the beautiful body God gave to you! Dress up! Go out!

In addition to the things I mentioned make sure you do what you love. Pursue your dreams. Continue to make goals. If you are passionate about it make sure you make time to do it.

Self Talk

Set the tone of your day with positive thoughts. Jot down some of your favorite sayings, readings, words, scriptures or quotes. Put them on your refrigerator, mirrors or planners and recite them. You should do this when you wake up in the morning or at night before you go to bed.

Reflect on the things you have rather than the things that you don't have. Count your blessings. Claim peace, joy, love, grace, mercy, protection, financial relief, good health, prosperity, success, hope and faith over your life. Think it. Feel it. Do it.

In life, each of us are faced with adversity. We all have our share of pain, struggles and disappointments. Many of these experiences cause trauma and can potentially lead to death similar to poison. An antidote neutralizes the effects of poison.

ABOUT THE AUTHOR

Ms. Snakecharma was born in Boston, MA on July 14th. Since birth she captivated many with her charisma. She is a certified administration specialist. Throughout her career as an admin she was trained and nationally certified as a coach and mentor. She took many leadership trainings, applied that knowledge and completed courses to become an instructor. She utilizes her education and coaching skills to provide edible feedback to her network. In addition, she works with entrepreneurs on personal development and streamlining businesses.

She loves sports, enjoys writing and appreciates good music. Outside of her career as an admin and educator she is a college radio host on Boston's legendary station 104.9FM WRBB. She partners with several businesses and provides resources on her platform and website.

Ms. Snakecharma decided to take the entrepreneurial leap by becoming Co-Founder/Owner of Unseen Handz Media. Unseen

Handz Media is a company that specializes in an array of services, including administration and publishing, both of which she is extremely passionate about. She published her first book "Daddy Issues" under her own imprint. "Daddy Issues" is now available on Amazon and www.unseenhandz.com. Although she has accomplished much Ms. Snakecharma has just begun her journey. She gives all thanks and glory to God.

Lightning Source UK Ltd.
Milton Keynes UK
UKHW020634160720
366640UK00014B/1315